BRUTON ENTERPRISES LLC

AVOID THE PITFALLS OF THE NACA MORTGAGE QUALIFICATION PROCESS

Learn the essential Do's and Don'ts to shorten the time frame it takes to qualify for a NACA Home Mortgage. Start building family wealth. Learn the best tips and secrets for a faster qualification.

First edition

This book was professionally typeset on Reedsy.
Find out more at reedsy.com

"Owning a home is a keystone of wealth—both financial affluence and emotional security." — Suze Orman

Contents

Introduction

We developed this book to help the many inspired home buyers to have the chance to become homeowners through NACA. However, due to NACA's eligibility requirements, policies, and procedures, many individuals are struggling to meet these standards or to qualify in a timely manner.

In addition, to assist any realtor in understanding the complexities of the NACA Home Mortgage process for their clients, they must guide them through the process efficiently. As a NACA-affiliated realtor, it is essential to know how to submit the necessary real estate documents promptly to NACA via your realtor portal to ensure a smooth closing for your client.

We are here to guide homebuyers and realtors through the essential Do's and Don'ts that can expedite the process of qualifying for a NACA Home Mortgage, helping buyers start building family wealth sooner. We'll share our top tips and insider secrets to help clients qualify for NACA more quickly.

Chapter 1: Before Thinking About Purchasing a Home, Get Your Mindset Together

Purchasing a home is a significant financial and emotional decision that requires a thoughtful and strategic mindset. Here are key aspects of the mindset you need:

1. Long-term Thinking

- Commitment to Stability: Buying a home typically involves settling in one location for several years. You should feel ready for this long-term commitment in terms of both your personal and financial goals.
- Future Planning: Consider how the home will fit your future life plans—family growth, career changes, or lifestyle needs.

2. Emotional Detachment

- Rational Decision-Making: Don't fall in love with a property too quickly. Approach the decision logically, considering whether it meets your needs and fits your budget.

- Patience: Finding the right home may take time, but waiting for favorable market conditions can save you significant money in the long run.

3. Flexibility

- Adaptability: Be open to compromises. You might not get everything on your wish list within your budget, so flexibility is critical when balancing needs and desires.

4. Resilience

- Facing Setbacks: You may encounter setbacks during the buying process (bidding wars, loan rejections), so resilience and persistence are necessary to keep moving forward.

5. Growth Mindset

- Investment Perspective: See homeownership as a personal milestone and a long-term investment. Understand that it takes time for property to appreciate and that it's a gradual wealth-building tool.

6. Community-Oriented Thinking

- Neighborhood Fit: Consider the community you're joining—does it align with your values, lifestyle, and long-term goals? Do you want to be in an HOA(Home Owners Association) community

Chapter 2: Before Thinking About Purchasing a Home, Get Your Finances Together

B e Financially Prepared

- **Budget Discipline:** Be prepared to live within a budget to save for managing the ongoing costs of homeownership (mortgage, maintenance, taxes, etc.). Start reducing your debt. NACA compares your debt to your income and determines your monthly mortgage. So, the less debt you have, the higher the mortgage you will receive.
  - **Credit Health:** NACA does not consider credit scores. They value your character, provided you've consistently paid your bills on time for at least 1 year.
  - **Emergency Funds:** Homeownership comes with unexpected expenses, so having a safety net for repairs or life events is vital.

Note: PLEASE DON'T PURCHASE ANYTHING EXPENSES WHILE GOING THROUGH ANY HOME MORTGAGE PROCESS.

Chapter 3: What is NACA

NACA (Neighborhood Assistance Corporation of America) is a non-profit organization that provides affordable homeownership opportunities to low- and moderate-income individuals and families. The NACA Homeownership Program offers a unique mortgage option with no down payment, no closing costs, no fees, no requirement for perfect credit, and below-market interest rates.

The primary goal of NACA is to make homeownership more accessible, particularly for people who may struggle to qualify for traditional mortgages. They offer extensive financial counseling to help potential buyers navigate home-buying and prepare them for homeownership.

NACA is known for its advocacy on behalf of underserved communities and for helping individuals build wealth through homeownership.

Chapter 4: How to Sign Up to NACA Homebuyer's Workshop

G o to naca.com
- Scroll down click: "Become a NACA homeowner"
- Click: "Get started with a workshop"
Choose English or Spanish Workshop

The first step in NACA's Purchase Program is to sign up for a free NACA Homebuyer Workshop. At this four-hour workshop, you will learn the details about the NACA program and the home-buying process. This includes detailed information to become NACA Qualified (i.e., mortgage ready).

You can attend a face-to-face workshop near you. NACA provides two workshops a month for each office, usually on a Saturday from 9:00 a.m. to 1:00 p.m. You can also take an online webinar workshop.

Once you complete the workshop, you will receive your NACA ID. You can then access your Member Portal to input your personal information and upload necessary documents.

TIP: You MUST stay the entire 4 hours because, at the end of the workshop, you will be given a NACA Code to access your NACA ID portal. If you leave, you will not get your NACA ID and may have to retake the workshop.

TIP: You CANNOT attend the NACA Homebuyer Workshop on your phone; you must be at a computer.

Note: Once you are NACA qualified to purchase a home, on a Thursday, you must attend the "Home Purchase Workshop." If you don't already have an outside affiliated NACA realtor, an in-house NACA Realtor will be assigned to you at the Purchase Workshop. However, if you already have an outside affiliated NACA Realtor, it's vital that your outside Realtor is known at the Home Purchase workshop.

Chapter 5: How Can NACA Assist You In Buying a Home?

N ACA is uniquely positioned to implement this transformative neighborhood stabilization program in collaboration with cities and towns. With over 30 years of experience, NACA has an outstanding track record, having closed more than 75,000 mortgages and maintaining a foreclosure rate of just 0.00012 (approximately one-hundredth of one percent). NACA is the leading organization for affordable homeownership, especially within minority communities.

Word-of-mouth recommendations from family, friends, neighbors, and coworkers further solidify NACA's position as the go-to source for affordable homeownership in these communities. The fact that more than 15,000 people begin the NACA process each month and that 10,000 to 20,000 people attend the multiday "Achieve the Dream" events serve as additional proof of this.

NACA provides its unprecedented Homeownership Programs in all fifty states, as described below.

- **Housing Counseling**
- **Homebuyer Purchase Program**
- **HOT-PHA(SECTION 8/Housing Choice Voucher)**
- **City One-Dollar Homeownership Program**
- **NACA'S New Construction Homes**
- **Homebuyer Purchase & Renovation Program**
- **Homeowners - Refinance & Renovation**
- **Homeowners - Home Save Program**
- **Rental Housing Program**

NACA BENEFITS FOR PURCHASING A HOME WITH THEM ARE:

- **NO DOWN PAYMENT**
- **NO CLOSING COST**
- **NO PMI(Private Mortgage Insurance)**
- **NO CREDIT SCORE CONSIDERATION**
- **BELOW-MARKET FIXED MORTGAGE RATE**
- **NO HIDDEN FEES WITH NACA**

WHAT NACA BUYERS PAY AT CLOSING: Homebuyers pay for the inspection, taxes, home insurance, maybe buyer broker, and HOA and buydown if applicable. Reserve Funds are set aside after closing for needed repairs.

Note: NACA's Homeownership Programs can be found and explained under the "Housing Programs" section of the "About" tab on the NACA website at naca.com.

Chapter 6: NACA Priority and Non-Priority Buyer Status

I n the NACA program, Priority Status refers to a designation given to homebuyers who meet specific criteria based on income and the area in which they are purchasing a home.

Specifically:

- **Priority Members** are buyers whose household income is below the median income for the Metropolitan Statistical Area (MSA) where they purchase a home. NACA prioritizes helping lower- to moderate-income individuals, so members with Priority Status may receive additional support and guidance to ensure successful homeownership.

- **Non-Priority Members** are buyers whose household income is above the median income for the MSA where they are buying. While these members can still take advantage of NACA's affordable mortgage program, they are encouraged to purchase homes in Targeted Areas (low- to moderate-income neighborhoods) to maintain the focus on neighborhood stabilization and economic development. They are required to use geomap.ffiec.gov/ffiecgeomap to qualify for the property.

The Priority Status plays a role in NACA's commitment to building wealth for underserved communities, and it can influence the types of neighborhoods where members are encouraged to buy homes.

Chapter 7: NACA Budget for Members

N ACA encourages its members to budget responsibly by focusing on financial discipline and demonstrating affordability for homeownership. Here are some key ways NACA wants members to budget:

1. Track Income and Expenses: Carefully monitor their monthly income and expenses to understand their financial situation and avoid unnecessary spending.
2. Establish Savings Habits: Save regularly, particularly toward the amount of their future mortgage payments. This demonstrates that they can afford homeownership and maintain financial stability.
3. Maintain Payment Shock Savings: NACA emphasizes the concept of "payment shock," which is the difference between current rent and the anticipated mortgage payment. Members are encouraged to save the amount equal to this difference each month to show they can handle the future mortgage.
4. Have Reserves: They must save enough to have reserves left in their bank accounts after closing on a property. This helps demonstrate long-term financial responsibility and ensures they are prepared for unexpected expenses.

5. Avoid Unnecessary Debt and Large Purchases: Avoid accumulating unnecessary debt and refrain from making large purchases during the qualification process, as it could negatively affect their financial standing and qualification status.

6. Use a Realistic Budget: They should live within their means, maintaining a budget that reflects their mortgage affordability and financial stability.

You are required to complete a monthly budget report BEFORE SEEING YOUR NACA MORTGAGE COUNSELOR.

TIP: If you regularly spend on grooming services (hair, nails, spa, etc.), it's crucial to stop these activities immediately. If NACA notices these charges on your credit card statements each month, they probably count it as a recurring expense. Instead, consider finding alternative ways to cover these costs without appearing on your statements. For example, you could borrow the money from someone and pay them back after your home purchase is finalized.

SECRET: Don't use your ATM card anymore while in the NACA process. Use your debit card at a grocery store for cash back. ATM cards show non-descriptive funds (deposit/withdrawal). NACA needs a description of those funds. Therefore, LOE will be required if you use your ATM card.

Chapter 8: What was Left Unsaid in the NACA Homebuyer's Workshop

What You Need to Do for NACA

Check all three of your Credit Bureaus for Certain specific Items that NACA will be examining.

The three major credit bureaus are Equifax, Experian, and TransUnion.

NACA doesn't care about your credit score; they are looking for the following items:

1. **Name Variation—Make** sure your name is exactly like it is when you sign up with NACA.
   Ex. Mary C. Sue (NACA has)
   Mary Sue (Creditors have) This must be corrected using NACA's LOE(Letters of Explanation) form
   OR
   Get the creditors to add the C to your name and update the credit report before you see your NACA's mortgage counselor.

2. Address Variation - The address NACA has must be the same on your Driver's License, and the creditors must have the same address. If not, write LOE to explain why the creditors have different addresses.

3. Check for Credit Inquiry - If you have any credit inquiries, you need to write LOEs

4. Bankruptcy - Chapter 7 or 13

- **Discharged:** Provide bankruptcy Documents including a cover page, summary of Schedules, Schedules A-J, Statement of debtor intent (If secured property is included in the bankruptcy), and discharge document. A Letter of Explanation outlining the circumstances that led to your bankruptcy, the reasons you believed bankruptcy was your only option, the steps you took to avoid it, and what actions you have taken to prevent a similar situation from happening in the future?
- **Dismissed:** Provide a Dismissal document and Letter of Explanation detailing what led to bankruptcy and why you could not complete it.

5. Liens/Judgement – .Provide documentation showing all liens or judgments have been satisfied/released. It must be recorded/released as documentation from the court or public records.

Note: Either resolve the issues on your credit report before meeting with your NACA Mortgage Counselor or be prepared to provide your Letters of Explanation (LOEs). If the problems remain unresolved, the process will be delayed, and the NACA Mortgage Counselor will give you an Action Plan to complete the LOEs. To avoid delays, complete the LOEs in advance and have them ready to submit. Hospital bills are not considered.

Chapter 9: Wait! Don't Hook Up Your Bank Account to NACA Yet

O rganize your bank statement(s) in a format similar to how NACA prefers it. Your bank statement(s) from your job payroll determines your monthly mortgage.

1. NACA requires 2 years of employment but will accept 1 year.
2. Only the Payroll from Your Primary Job(s) determines your monthly mortgage.

TIPS:

1. If you have a full-time job for over a year and a part-time job for less than a year, the part-time income won't be considered when determining your monthly mortgage. However, you can use the part-time income for shock payment or to buy down the interest rate. DO NOT PLACE THE PART TIME INCOME IN THE BANK ACCOUNT WHERE YOUR FULL TIME PAYROLL IS GOING. KEEP THEM IN SEPARATE ACCOUNTS(Checking/Savings). ONLY KEEP THE PAYROLL MONEY THAT DETERMINES YOUR NACA MONTHLY MORTGAGE IN AN ACCOUNT BY ITSELF. DON'T MIX THE FUNDS. This makes it easier for the NACA Mort-

gage Counselor to determine your monthly mortgage accurately.

1. If you bank at more than 2 banks and your payroll goes to so many accounts, DON'T DO THAT. Your NACA counselor is very business and doesn't have the time to follow your payroll account to determine your monthly mortgage. Use the KISS method. Try to get down to 1 no more than 2 banks. If not, you probably will get a lower monthly mortgage amount.

Ideally, NACA likes to see your primary payroll go into a bank account (ex. checking), and see all of your bills paid from that account. **TIP**: PLEASE DO NOT TRANSFER ANY REMAINING FUNDS FROM YOUR CHECKING ACCOUNT TO YOUR SAVINGS ACCOUNT. KEEP THE EXTRA MONEY IN YOUR CHECKING ACCOUNT. IT CAN BE CONSIDERED SHOCK PAYMENT.

TIPS:

1. No Zelle, Cashapp, Venom, or any other bank app like these in your primary account when NACA determines your mortgage. Using those apps, you CANNOT send or receive from anyone in your primary account. Now, if you are paying rent or some bill monthly with these bank app, then that's acceptable with NACA because it's consistent. If your bank statement shows bank app-related transactions, AVOID sharing that statement with NACA. **TIP:** Instead, wait and provide the following month's statement after

19

clearing the transactions.
2. Save money, as you must have reserves remaining in your bank account after closing on a property.

Note: Upload to your member portal monthly bank statements, payroll, and credit cards UNTIL YOU CLOSE ON YOUR HOME. NEVER STOP UPLOADING UNTIL YOU CLOSE ON YOUR HOME.

Make a Difference with Your Review

Unlock the Power of Generosity

"The best way to find yourself is to lose yourself in the service of others." – Mahatma Gandhi

People who give without expecting anything in return often feel more joy. Your review can help someone just like you—eager to buy a home but unsure how to start with NACA.

I wrote *Avoid the Pitfalls of the NACA Mortgage Qualification Process* to make this journey easier and less stressful for everyday people. But in order to help more future homeowners, I need a little help from readers like you.

Would You Leave a Review?

Many people choose what to read based on what others say. Your voice matters.

Leaving a review takes less than a minute, but it could change someone's homeownership journey.

Your words could help...

...a first-time buyer finally get their home.

...a family avoid costly delays.

...a hard-working couple save time and stress.

...a hopeful dreamer believe they can do it too.

Just scan the QR code or click this link:

If you love helping others, then you're my kind of person.

Thank you from the bottom of my heart!

— Phyllis Buck

Chapter 10: What's Shock Payment and How Does It Work?

An additional amount of money that NACA requires potential homebuyers to save each month, demonstrating their financial discipline and readiness for homeownership. This is often used when a borrower wants to qualify for a mortgage with a payment higher than what they currently pay in rent.

Here's how it works:

- Current Housing Payment: NACA assesses how much you currently pay for rent or other housing costs.
- Desired Mortgage Payment: NACA calculates the estimated monthly mortgage payment based on the home price you're aiming for.
- Shock Payment Amount: If the estimated mortgage payment is higher than your current rent, NACA may ask you to save the difference consistently each month. This is called a shock payment.

For example:

- If you're paying $1,000 in rent but want a mortgage with a $1,500 monthly payment, NACA will require you to save the $500 difference each month as a "shock payment" to show that you can handle the higher cost. This $500 can ONLY be from your payroll and no other funds.

The idea behind the shock payment is to ensure that you're financially capable of handling the higher mortgage payment and to build up your savings, which could be used for unexpected expenses or future housing costs.

TIP: Stocks, bonds, and 401 (k) Retirement Accounts can help you purchase a house. You must let your mortgage counselor know ASAP and get funds ready ASAP. Write a Commitment LOE Letter (for funds you are contributing to your 401K or Retirement Accounts from your payroll) indicating that (Your contributions to these funds are voluntary and that, if you need them to make your mortgage payment, you are willing to stop them in whole or in part and divert them to meet your housing payment).

Chapter 11: NACA HANDS DEPARTMENT (Home And Neighborhood Development Standards)

I n NACA (Neighborhood Assistance Corporation of America), **HANDS** stands for **Home and Neighborhood Development Standards**. It's a department within NACA that plays a critical role in ensuring that the properties NACA members purchase are safe, livable, and meet NACA's minimum property condition standards.

Here's how HANDS works in the NACA process, especially in relation to home inspections and dealing with inspectors:

Role of HANDS in Property Review

Once you're under contract on a home, NACA requires you to hire a licensed home inspector who is affiliated with NACA —but not connected to the seller. You will pay for this inspection, which aims to assess the property's condition.

- The inspection report must be submitted to NACA.
- HANDS reviews this report to identify any **health and safety concerns** or **repair issues** that could impact livability or lead to significant costs after purchase.

Required vs. Recommended Repairs

HANDS will categorize repairs into two types:

- **REQUIRED REPAIRS**: These must be completed before closing or escrowed (set aside as funds for post-closing repairs) if eligible. Examples include:
- Roof damage
- Foundation problems
- Electrical hazards
- Broken heating systems

1. Your Realtor should be able to negotiate with the Seller to make the required repairs prior to closing. If the Seller does not agree to pay for the required repairs, the NACA buyer must ensure they have sufficient funds available in their monthly budget to cover the repairs.
2. If the required repair costs are covered by the Seller and funds are given to the NACA buyer at closing, the buyer must perform the repairs and have the NACA inspector return for a re-inspection.
3. If the required repair is at a small cost (e.g., $100), it's better to have the addendum state that the $100 is going towards the buyer's closing costs and prepaid rather than mentioning the repair. It's easier for HANDS to clear the property.

4. Request a **repair escrow**, where money is set aside from the mortgage to make the repairs after closing (only available for certain repairs and must be under a $10,000 cap, subject to lender approval). The HANDS team may also approve or deny escrow requests based on their guidelines.
5. You **cannot proceed to bank application** (credit access) until the HANDS department has approved the inspection report and repair plan (if applicable).
6. If HANDS flags major issues and you can't resolve them, you may be advised to walk away from the property.

- **RECOMMENDED REPAIRS**: These are suggested but not mandatory. They may affect comfort or long-term value, but they don't pose an immediate risk. They don't affect the closing of the property.

Here's a **sample checklist** of what NACA's **HANDS department** typically looks for when reviewing a home inspection report. These are focused on **health, safety, and structural integrity**—not cosmetic issues.

NACA HANDS – Sample Property Condition Checklist

Structural and Safety

- **Roof**: No leaks, sagging, missing shingles, or damage
- **Foundation**: No cracks, shifting, or water intrusion
- **Floors**: Solid and level—no soft spots or trip hazards
- **Stairs/Railings**: Secure handrails, safe treads, no rot
- **Ceilings/Walls**: No major cracks, water stains, or mold

Electrical System

- **Electrical Panel**: Properly labeled, no corrosion or overheating
- **Wiring**: No exposed wires or outdated knob-and-tube
- **Outlets/Switches**: Functional and grounded, especially in kitchens/bathrooms (GFCI required)
- **Smoke/CO Detectors**: Working in key areas (kitchen, bedrooms, hallways)

Plumbing

- **Water Heater**: Functional, no leaks, proper pressure relief valve
- **Visible Pipes**: No active leaks or corrosion
- **Water Flow**: Adequate water pressure in sinks, tubs, toilets
- **Drainage**: Proper drainage from all fixtures; no standing water
- **Sewer/Septic**: In good condition and tested if applicable

Doors and Windows

- **Windows**: Open/close properly, no cracked panes, adequate seals
- **Doors**: Lock properly, weather-tight, including entry and interior doors
- **Egress**: Bedrooms must have a means of emergency escape (usually a window)

Exterior and Site

- **Siding/Exterior Walls**: No rot, damage, or large cracks
- **Gutters/Drainage**: Functional and directing water away from foundation
- **Driveways/Walkways**: No major trip hazards or broken slabs
- **Garage/Outbuildings**: Structurally sound and secure

Pests and Mold

- **Pest Inspection**: No active infestation (termites, rodents, etc.)
- **Mold**: No visible mold or signs of hidden water damage

Life Safety

- **Stairs & Railings**: Secure, especially exterior and basements
- **Emergency Egress**: Windows in all bedrooms, functional exits
- Lead **Paint** (for homes built before 1978): Assessed or disclosed

Tip:

The **home inspection report** should include:

- Clear descriptions
- Photographs of issues
- Recommendations from the inspector

Chapter 12: NACA Mortgage Counselors, Realtors and Inspectors

MORTGAGE COUNSELORS
Assigned to NACA member after 3 months of portal uploads (payroll, bank statements, credit card statements, etc.)
TIP: Both spouses must attend the First Intake with the NACA Mortgage Counselor. No exceptions!

REALTORS

Must sign up online and attend a 2 hr webinar to be affiliated with NACA. Afterwards, they are given a realtor portal. It's important that you know the NACA procedure well to prevent a delayed closing for your NACA client. Documents must be uploaded to NACA ASAP. Ask your NACA buyer for the contact information of their mortgage counselor. Introduce yourself to your buyer's Mortgage Counselor immediately.

Signup: naca.com

    Go to vendor, drop down and select real estate agent

    Go to Not Registered, Sign up.

    Complete Realtor Information & Create a password.

    Go back to naca.com and sign up for RED Intro to NACA webinar:

    Homebuyers Tab, Live Webinars, Tuesday

TIP: Once your client has been qualified to purchase a home by NACA, promptly obtain the contact information for an approved NACA inspector and a NACA-approved closing firm from the Mortgage Counselor. Termite inspector doesn't need to be NACA approved. Please ensure that the Termite Inspector's Report is uploaded to your NACA portal.NACA portal. After your offer is accepted, allow 35 days for closing. You should immediately complete a Transaction Summary Form for NACA to initiate the transaction processing for your client. Without this form, NACA will not have any information about the contract. Upload both the Executed Purchase Contract and the Transaction Summary to NACA through your portal as soon as possible. Contact the NACA inspector to schedule an inspection right away. During the inspection, the client must be present for a photo, which the inspector will upload along with the inspection report to NACA.

TIP: Address the results of the inspection report as you normally would, but keep in mind that speed is crucial with NACA. Prepare any necessary addendum based on the findings of the inspection. You may need to work with the NACA HAND Department (Home and Neighborhood Development), which reviews the inspector's report and determines the required actions, similar to what a Realtor would assess.

INSPECTORS

The inspector must be NACA-affiliated by completing an inspector's webinar. The inspector must take a picture of the NACA member in front of the property. Therefore, members are required to attend the inspection.

TIP: If a buyer knows an inspector, they can have the inspector sign up for the NACA Inspector's webinar. This needs to be done well in advance before the offer is accepted.

Chapter 13: More NACA Tips and Secrets

S TUDENT LOAN
Before seeing your NACA Mortgage Counselor, you must obtain a form from student services stating the amount you owe and the month and year you will start paying. If you have been forgiven, you need proof. Get the paperwork from student services.

CHILD SUPPORT/ALIMONY

You must upload the child(s) birth certificate. Child support doesn't count towards your monthly mortgage, so don't place the funds in the job payroll primary account(checking). Don't mingle the funds. Place them in another account(savings). Provide court documents proving benefits are being received. Both can be used towards MRF and buying down the interest rate.

CHILDREN OVER 21 AND LIVE AT HOME

SECRET: Just don't tell the Mortgage Counselor. It's a headache. They, too, would have to submit paperwork to NACA just like you if they are working.

DIVORCE

Upload divorce decree papers to your portal. Include all pages and all articles.

WORKING AND GETTING PAID WITH CASH

Unless you file taxes with the cash, you have no income.

MARRIED

Even if your spouse is not interested in purchasing a home, they must still be listed on the account. Both spouses must upload the necessary paperwork, and their combined income and debt will be considered. Therefore, if you are in the process of a divorce, it is essential to finalize the divorce before proceeding.

YEARLY TAXES

Provide tax transcripts and tax returns for 2 years.

UNMARRIED BUT LIVING WITH SOMEONE AND DESIRE TO BUY A HOME

Splitting the household expenses. NACA has to see you save your monthly mortgage desired amount for 6 months from your primary job's payroll after your monthly bills are paid. Then, continue to save this amount until you close on your home. Additionally, a letter from the house's owner or your name on the lease, confirming your contribution to monthly household expenses or rent, must be provided as proof.

NACA FEES

NACA fees are due on January 1 of the year. So, if you started in November or December and paid dues, you must pay again on January 1st of the new year. So, you figure it out. Wait until January of the following year to first pay NACA dues.

NACA PARTICIPATION

NACA mandates that you participate. Can do for participation: social media post on your personal Facebook, create a poster in Canva about NACA (pdf file) to share with people, volunteer at a NACA office. LOE letter about a signed-up NACA member(s) you told them about NACA and they signed up and got a NACA ID. Provide their NACA ID.

ELIGIBILITY WITH PREVIOUS PROPERTY

Provide proof of how each property was disposed of. If the property was sold, provide the HUD-1. If the property was foreclosed upon, provide the Sheriff of Sale or Deed Under Power with the verification of the foreclosure date. Can't have another property at the time of closing on a NACA property.

GRANTS

Must already be approved before getting qualified with NACA. The grant approval amount will be added to your funds. You search for your grants. Ask your NACA counselor about grants, too.

MULTI-UNIT PROPERTY

Must take the Landlord NACA webinar.

Conclusion

Keeping the Game Alive

Now that you've got the tools to make the NACA process smoother, faster, and way less frustrating, it's your turn to shine the light for others.

By leaving a review, you help future homebuyers find this guide—and avoid the same mistakes. Your honest feedback shows others that there *is* a clear path forward through NACA's maze of rules and steps.

Help Someone Take the First Step

Think of how far you've come. Now think of someone else just starting out—confused, overwhelmed, and maybe even ready to give up.

Your review might be the very thing that gives them hope.

Click below to leave your review on Amazon:

☞ https://www.amazon.com/review/review-your-purchases/ ?asin=BOOKASIN

Thank you again. *Avoid the Pitfalls of the NACA Mortgage Qualification Process* keeps making a difference because of generous readers like you.

— *Phyllis Buck*

We hope the insights and secrets shared here empower you to pursue your dreams of homeownership confidently and help you navigate the National Association for the Advancement of Homeownership (NACA) program. The NACA program is a powerful tool for those who qualify, but it requires commitment, patience, and attention to detail.

For further support, we invite you to join our NACA Facebook group, where like-minded buyers share encouragement and tips on their journey to homeownership.

Please join our NACA Facebook Community (https://www.face book.com/groups/nacainformationsupportgroup).

If you found this book helpful, please leave us a favorable Amazon review. Happy Househunting from us to you!

Resources

ACA Official Website

NACA. (2000). *NACA*. https://www.naca.com/. Retrieved October 12, 2024, from https://www.naca.com/

Facebook Group

Link: [https://www.facebook.com/groups/nacainformationsupportgroup]

Recommended Reading

NACA Qualification Workbook

www.ingramcontent.com/pod-product-compliance
Lightning Source LLC
Chambersburg PA
CBHW071215301125
36101CB00043B/1913